The reflections
Of a bruised heart

Whitney Hodge

The reflections Of a bruised heart

Whitney Hodge

Whitney Hodge

The Reflections Of A Bruised Heart

Copyright © 2020 by Whitney Hodge.

All rights reserved. No part of this book may be reproduced or transmitted in any form or by any means, electronic or mechanical, including photocopying, recording, or by any information storage and retrieval system, without permission in writing from the copyright author, except for the use of brief quotations in a book review.

Library of Congress Cataloging-In-Publication Data

Name: Hodge, Whitney, author.
Title: The Reflection Of A Bruised Heart / Whitney Hodge

Identifiers:
LCCN:
ISBN: 978-1-970135-69-5 Paperback

Published in the United States by
Pen2Pad Ink Publishing
www.pen2padink.org.

Requests to publish work from this book or to contact the author should be sent to: whitneyrhodge@gmail.com

Whitney Hodge

The Reflections Of A Bruised Heart

Contents

1. Dedication — 9
2. Forever Waiting — 12
3. I See You — 14
4. My Long Goodbye — 16
5. Peace — 17
6. A Sister's Heart — 19
7. Torn — 21
8. Never Be — 22
9. Another Mother — 24
10. IDK — 25
11. I Love My Friends — 27
12. Blessing — 29
13. Heart Of Pain — 30
14. Sunshine — 32
15. Endless Friendship — 34
16. A Letter For You — 36
17. Running — 38
18. I Bet! — 40
19. So Not Funny — 42
20. Shade — 45
21. Keep It Real — 48
22. Sad Days — 50
23. Last Time Was The Last Time — 52
24. To My Unborn — 56
25. You Ain't — 58

26. Honest 61
27. I Miss My Auntie 63
28. Auntie Shannon 64
29. Death 65
30. Lucky Little Me 67
31. A Letter to Depression And Anxiety 69
32. You 71
33. Story Time 72
34. About The Author 77
35. Get Connected 78

Dedication

This book is dedicated to my
two aunties who passed away.

Donna Hodge
Jan. 17, 1961 – May 24, 2019

Shannon Harper
Jan. 31, 1973 – June 10, 2019

Whitney Hodge

*Be yourself
unapologetically*

Whitney Hodge

Forever Waiting

So you say you miss me,
because you never get to see me
You say I make you smile
even when there are miles
Between us
You say you like when I'm around
so you can wrap
Your arms around me
You also said I'm fun, I'm funny, and cute
But I have one question;
what's left for me to do
You got me jumping through
all these hoops
I guess you would like the moon
and for me to bring it
To you on a silver spoon
You said you can't leave me alone
but yet I'm so alone
All the people call my phone
I tell them to go on
Cause I'm waiting on a call
But I never get that call
now my head is against the Wall
Now I'm thinking, yea I've been thinking
Maybe I should give up on this
Yea I'm giving up on this

The Reflections Of A Bruised Heart

Then you send me a text with emoji
saying you miss me
I can't help but reply
I miss you too
The way you got me feeling
I don't know what to do
I just want to be with you
This love got me so confused
If I make you happy and
I make you smile and you
misses me when I'm not around
Why am I feeling so down
You're the reason I can't sleep at night
You are the reason
my heart don't beat right
I messed up and I can't be with you
But I'll be forever waiting on you

Whitney Hodge

I See You

I see you
That smile on your face
Behind the make-up and hair spray
The anger in the words you say
I see you

You're just a girl finding her way
Never asking for help because your pride is in the way
Never accepting love because you're afraid it will fade away
I see you

The sadness behind your eyes
I know some nights you cry
I know you wonder why life has to be so hard at times
I see you

Afraid to love afraid to trust never truly wanting to give your heart up
That's why you have built a wall so high so you'll always have tour guard up
I see you

Despite all the things you do and all the things you say despite that

The Reflections Of A Bruised Heart

Smile on your face
I know you've been looking for love in
every single place
So don't worry I see you

My Long Goodbye

It was fun while it lasted
The laughs we had were classic
The time we spent will be sent to the back
of my head and turned into
memories of passion
I will remember your smile and
how it drives me wild
But I can no longer stand on the sideline
and watch this time fly by
When I could be preparing for my guy
Who has that twinkle in his eye
That's gonna love me till we die
I'd admit I thought it was you
But if I was to wait on you,
I'll be turning blue
I'm just looking for something true
I really hoped it was you
But I won't be played for a fool
So I have to cut you lose

Peace!!!

Don't come at me in that way
With all that anger in your face
With them harsh words you love to say
Of course I moved on
You the one that left home
Like a fool I begged you to stay I can't lie I even prayed
But them days has faded away
I'll admit I'm glad to say
I don't need you for anything these days
So you trying to come back is a waste of time
do I need to rewind and remind you of
All the things you put me through
I'm so happy I'm through with you
Since you were so quick to bell out
Get your bags and sail OUT!

Whitney Hodge

*Take a break
and live!*

A Sister's Heart

When I was born you were six
When I was six you made me sick
When I was eight the feelings that I had for you was hate
When I was nine I was so blind to all the things that was happening in our time
Mama working three jobs
Our brother was running the streets hard
Daddy who knows where he goes because the drugs had him
So that left me and you

I didn't know how fast you had to grow
I thought you hated me with all your soul
You were 15 and hate was all you showed
But that's all you known
Because when I look back we had some fun but a lot of pain
It was some sun but a lot of rain
It wasn't until the year 2000
We was hit with a lot of pain
When you was shot in the ear from a far range
It wasn't until then I seen the love you had for me
It wasn't until then I understood the word

tragedy
At that moment you took back every mean thing you done to me
At that moment I prayed that God wouldn't take you away from me
See I really didn't hate you
I really just wanted you to be okay
So I prayed and God made a way

Because if you would've died that day
I would've never been okay
And I know this sound crazy
but I would never take that day away
That day was a blessing in disguise
That day really opened our eyes
We are so much closer now
You're more than my sister
We are more like best friends
I wouldn't trade you for all the money in the world because who would I spend it with
You are my sister, my friend, and I will love you till the end of time.

Dedicated to Stacy Hodge

The Reflections Of A Bruised Heart

Torn between the two!
Who love is really true?
Torn between the eyes!
Who beauty lies deep inside?
Torn between the emotions!
Who has the deeper devotion?
Torn between the voices!
Who words burn like torches?
Torn between the touch!
Who gives me that feeling in my gut?
Is it you or is it you?
I'm so torn between the two that I don't
know what to do!

Whitney Hodge

Never Be

I'm drawn to you like a pencil to a notepad
I wish we never did it because now it's all bad
Only been knowing you for some weeks
But your smell be having me weak
Your lips knock me off my feet
I try to fight it but I surrender in defeat
Being with you makes me complete
But us being together could never be
Your voice reminds me of a sad song
We could never be, we could never be
keeps playing in my head like a bad song melody
Lying next to you is where I'd rather be
My head on your chest up against your breast
Counting your every breath is paradise at its best
But we have ended before we ever started
We have been forced into a friend zone our feelings discarded
Because I am here and you are there
It's no way we could ever be a pair

*Never compromise
Who you are to make
Someone else happy!*

Whitney Hodge

Another Mother

Another mother can't you see
Another mother he granted just for me
You were there to wipe my tears
You showed me how to conquer my fears
By my side when I was alone
Taught me things right and wrong
Told me I should never hide
Taught me how to walk with pride
The best parts about me I learned from you
I know it seems we're far apart
But your love has never left my heart
I know it seems I'm not the same
But you have been a great mother and I won't complain
We go through our ups and downs
But best believe I'm going to stick around
You were there for me from the start
So I love you, love you with all my heart
I hope you know my love is real
But you're like my BFF Jill

Dedicated to A'besa Hodge

IDK

I don't know why I feel this way
I don't know why my smile won't stay
I don't know why I'm empty inside
I don't know why some nights I cry
I don't know why I feel this pain
I don't know how to make a change
Tell me why I feel so strange
Even the days I feel so high my heart sometimes feel likes it wants to cry
And if you understand how I feel than you know these words are real
A deep depression makes me wanna pop some pills
And I can't lie I even tried because this pain has never left my side
But dying is not an option of mine because I'm dead inside
I walk these streets I meet and great with a smile on my face that you can't beat
But I feel no love I have no shame just carrying this heavy burden of pain
I'm so lost and I'm so confused
Somebody tell me what should I do
Around and round I go but this feeling inside just won't go
Living this life of heart ache and pain how

Whitney Hodge

could I remain the same
I have lived my whole life with pain
I have come accustomed to feeling so drained
I feel like I'm walking through a lifetime of rain
I don't know why I feel this way

I Love My Friends

We laugh together
We cry together
We might as well die together
Because if you leave this world before I do
My life would be nothing without you
Your apart of me and I'm apart of you
A bond that last forever
We stick harder than glue
Tighter than a knot on the string of a shoe
Closer than two peas in a pond
How could I ever forget about you?
Blood or no blood we are related
Our jokes never get out dated
So no matter the time apart this friendship is forever

I was blessed to be

loved by you…

Blessings

When I hold your hand my heart begins to dance
When I look into your eyes I pray this love never dies
Like I can't get you out my mind no matter the time
Your soul has connected with mine and our souls has intertwined
You injected your love into to me like a vaccine for pain
Since the day I laid eyes on you I haven't been the same
You saved my life and you changed my world
You're a blessing no disguise
I will forever lift my eyes
And thank God
for the time we spent

Whitney Hodge

Heart Of Pain

It's not you it's me I promise
Sometimes me heart is to reminded
Of all the people who left and never came back
The few who said they had my back
 instead they used a knife to stab me like that
The ones who stayed but never showed a care in the world
The ones who went to the grave and left me in this cold, cold world
Everyone who cared for me they opened up their eyes to see
 The person I turned out to be
Then they turned their backs and talked
Against me quicker than my enemies
Reminded of every "I LOVE YOU"
that fell from the lips of a LIAR
All the harsh words that burn like fire
Every embrace that lasted longer than a minute
While connected to a person who was never committed
So I'll admit it all these people left scars on my heart
And time hasn't sealed these scars

from being revealed
So I'm uncertain and it's running through my veins
So When You Say "I love you" and
I say "I love you too"
It's just not the same

Sunshine

You are my sunshine
But you are my rain
You bring me joy
But you give me Pain
I want the world to know
But you are ashamed
I want to love you for a lifetime
But you don't feel the same

Brenda Oritz is my best friend, and when we found out she would be stationed in Germany for 3 years we were both sad. I wrote this and sent it to her while she was boarding the airplane.

I love that woman; she was the first person I came out to. She was one of the few people who didn't care and told me to not worry about anybody to be happy no matter what.

Whitney Hodge

Endless Friendships

5, 411.47 miles won't keep me away from
Remember that my love is always true
Remember that this friendship is real
3 years is not a long time it's no big deal
I'm only a phone call away and I have a
 Million silly jokes that will brighten your day
I shall hold on to these memories
Till I'm old and grey and I pray they never fade away
5,411.47 miles that's a long drive
But my love will follow you wherever you go it won't hide
So carry my spirit around with you
I'm embedded in your soul
We are meant to be together and grow old
I have faith in you I love you and I hope it shows
5,411.47 miles that's how far you will be from me
So stop and hold me tight so I'm always in your memory
You're my BREN these miles are not the end
So this is a see you later
We don't do goodbyes

The Reflections Of A Bruised Heart

Even though as I write these tears fill my eyes
I know one day you will make it back to me
And to your arms I will run
Where I forever want to be

A Letter For You

You knew I liked you from the start
With a Pen my feelings flow from my heart
But standing with you here face to face
I can never find the words to say
Been holding these feelings for a min
Never was the place or time to spill it
Never thought you would feel it or was stilling feeling me
So I wrote this letter just to see
If you were like me and wished we worked it out
Or took it slow so the spark didn't burn out
So I pour my heart into your hands
In hopes that we can make a mends
I never really had a plan
I just hoped this letter reaches your hands

Situationship –

A friendship that's more than a friendship but not a relationship.

Whitney Hodge

Running

I was running so fast I destroyed everything in my path
Every relationship and **situationship** I was in I destroyed it
I destroyed it all because I was running and I couldn't slow down
Because she was after me and
She knows my past, my darkest secrets and how bad I could be
So I ran because if she ever caught me it could be a tragedy,
A catastrophe only God knows what she had in store for me and I had no intentions of trying to see
So I was running
Running into hurt people
Hurting them more
Running into broken people
Breaking them more
Running into situations I can't get out of
Didn't have time to stop and be loved
And I been running so long I feel like I was losing myself
And I'm not the type to stop and ask for help
But I can't stop thinking about the past

itself so I had to stop and ask myself
How bad was this person I was running from and it wasn't until
Then I realize it was **ME** the whole time that I was running from
The hardest part about letting go of you is
 Leaving behind the part of me I gave to you

I Bet!

When she asked you about me, I BET you told her we were just friends
I BET you didn't tell her you still love me deep within
I BET she don't know I was the one who broke your heart and
It's impossible for us to be apart
I BET she didn't know I'm the one who picks you up when she puts you down
And I'm the one you run to when she's not around
I BET she doesn't know you're doing it for the gram and doing it for the likes
Does she really know what crosses your mind at night?
I bet she can't even feed your soul and will she push you toward your dreams and goals
And does she know about them late night phone calls I BET she don't
Would she forgive you for those deleted messages I BET she won't?
Does she know that she's just the next chick trying to fill that void I left you with?
I hold them pieces to your puzzle to make you whole so

Replacing me is a goal she could never reach
Does she know that she's just temporary like a fake tattoo, but?
that's your job to tell her not me and I BET YOU WON'T

So Not Funny

You know what's funny to me
The whole time I was chasing you I was losing me and I didn't even know it
Trying to please you while letting go of everything I stood for
Because I thought I loved you and you loved me
But you only needed me to get you through those lonely nights
Because when I was out of your sight, I was out of your mind
And you were out chasing the next hot young thing trying to bump and grind
See I'm older now and I don't respect that and I don't respect you
The nerve of you to tell me I'm going to be a lonely fool
Well I rather be a lonely fool than a fool for you
See I trusted you put my heart into your hands and you played me like kids play in the sand
And I was taught to **NEVER TRUST A MAN**
But I didn't I trusted love and I was taking for granted the fool I am again

The Reflections Of A Bruised Heart

Love has tarnish and diminished my grin took my love and played kick ball with its friends
You ever had a feeling you never gone be whole again
That's how I'm feeling and that feeling will never be comfortable to me
And I will never be comfortable with being second to these freaks or second to these streets
SO, if loving you is right, I don't mind being wrong
because I was brought into this world by myself so I don't mind being alone

SHADE - *Acting in a casual or disrespectful manner.*

Shade

Are you mad or nah?
Because honestly, I'm glad you are gone
You came and got your backpack and your night sack and now
You say you're moving on
BUT you still creep my post and watch my snaps
You still follow me on the gram just to see how I am
I'm doing good if you ask me but you, you are not gone never get passed me
Trying to make me jealous with your new little shawty
Oh, I see you're getting trashy
She's like a ring pop, I'm more like a diamond ring
She's cute, she's cheap
Me I'm more like designer things
She doesn't require much of you
I require the finer things
And it's not all about the money I'm just trying to give you an example of who I'm trying to be
You couldn't feed me mentally, you couldn't feed my soul

Whitney Hodge

You lack intellect, morals, and goals
You like to play high school games, and wear high school clothes
And I'm not trying to put you down I'm just trying to let you know
We want two different things, we are driving in two different lanes
I can't do it all on my own so it's time for a change
"What's the code on yo phone" "No what's the code on y….."
See who got time to play those type of games
So, if you want to chase hotties and run after thotties be my guest
Cause honestly, I was always out of your league
And when you come to your senses remember
God give second chances he still working on me

Be with someone who's not afraid to love you.

Keep It Real

You said you wanted someone to take care of your heart
But you couldn't even keep it real from the start
You never wanted someone that would treat you right
You looked over me and picked the same ole type
The same ole kind
The same type of person who leaves you crying
That can never be faithful and never tell you the truth
You stepped on my poor little heart just to be played like a fool
Not you looking at me like "what should I do"
I just laugh cause now the fool is you
She should have made a better decision at the beginning
When you picked her over me that was our ending?
So, get off my phone singing them old sad songs
Oh, you don't remember you was the one who did me wrong

The Reflections Of A Bruised Heart

And I have moved on and you can't try to
Found your way back like a boomerang
Keep calling my phone calling me boo and things
And I be acting like am busy like I'm doing things
Cause I'm OVER YOU
But you keep coming from my past like you overdue
I asked you one simple question
And you LIED
If it would've been life and death
I would've died
So how am I suppose trust you with my achy breaky heart
When you couldn't keep it real from the start

Sad Days

Every day I have cried because I knew this was coming to an end
Every day I lied and said I was happy when I held the truth so deep down within
Every day I cried because I wanted to be loved so exceptional
Every day I lied and said our love was unconventional
Every day I cried because I went through everything my mom told me not to
Every day I lied and I told her We was doing well when she asked about you
Every day I was a ticking time bomb ready to explode
Carrying all these emotions like a hand gun ready to unload
Every day I waited like a puzzle for you to make me whole
Every day you looked at me I watched your love fade away
Every day I looked at you I gave a little more of myself away hoping that you would stay
Every day was a rollercoaster didn't know which way was up or down
Every day I lost a little trust

Until finally one day
I just gave up

Whitney Hodge

Last Time Was The Last Time

I told you I was broken
You said you could fix me
I told you I would never love again
You told me time heals everything
But I replied not this time
Because last time was the last time
I would settle for less
Last time was the last time I would give a person my best
Last time was the last time I would pack my bags and leave
Last time was the last time a person could treat me like I was second string
My heart was broken for the last time
I've been hopeless for the last time
I fell for a person just like you last time
And I see too much of them in you
So, this is something I can't do
And I know you only want to me better than I was loved before
But I got to pick up these pieces of me and put them back together and it'd not easy
And I'm not holding you accountable for

what happened in my past
And I love that you love me but you're moving too fast
And last time was the last time I will ignore any signs

I'm sorry if you're waiting
but I'm not over last time

I wasn't loyal to you because of who you are

I was loyal because that's who I am

Whitney Hodge

To My Unborn

Dear child
I cried for you today,
the thought of never meeting you is over crowding my thoughts.
The thought of never receiving that love from you makes me sad.
I know you would've been awesome and amazing.
I don't know if I will ever get a chance to meet you but I love you!
Maybe I'm not fit to be a mother to you or maybe you were given to someone who needed you more,
maybe I want you for the wrong reasons. But I know even if you don't end up with me I know you will turn out wonderful and I hope
Your life is full of so much love.

I'm sorry if I hurt you and I regret not loving you. Watching you love someone else is sickening

Whitney Hodge

Ain't

You ain't never had to ask me for shit
Because if I had it was yours
I've gave you my last dime on a few
occasions in return you gave me grief
You gave me a cold shoulder
I couldn't cry on
You gave me advice I couldn't use
And excuses I didn't need
I would give you my last and you wouldn't
give me half of what you had
I gave you my listening ears to unload all of
your insecurities and worries about life
And in my absence, you wouldn't even put
up a fight for me
I gave you love like you never received
In return you gave me a broken heart that
doesn't come with
A factory warranty and
Insecurities that I can't get rid of
You took time I didn't have to give
I wasted a lot of time
A lot of love and
 A lot of tears all on you
And all I have to show for it is these scars
that I'm left with and
This baggage full of worries and fear,

insecurities, and pain
Everything I did for you

You wouldn't do the same
The crazy part about it
you won't miss me until I'm gone
But then there's no coming back
This really saddens me because I
always had your back

The Reflections Of A Bruised Heart

Honest

To Be Honest
I'm just taking a break for me
Taking a break to breathe
Taking a break to see if I can actually get back to the happy me
My friends say I changed idk I feel the same
Just taking a break from being ashamed of all the Hurt, lies, and pain
Life is getting a little heavy so I'm taking a break for me
Taking a break from listening to everyone's problems
Taking a break from being the solver

My shoulder needs a break from being cried on because it's all cried out
My hands need a break from putting the pieces back together
Because there's too many on my plate
My mind is tired from being the anchor that's holding your ships in place
My back has begun to hurt from holding everyone's weight

I'm really sorry I'll be back soon
Don't come looking for me I'm in my break

Whitney Hodge

room
When you leave
Leave everything on the table you left
I don't like leftovers

I Miss My Auntie

The laughter and love we had was pure and came with ease
Our hearts were saddened the day you had to leave
The only thing that helps the thought of you being gone
Is knowing you have found a resting place of your own
With no more pain and no more sorrow and
You no longer have to worry about tomorrow
A place to heal and conquer your fears
I found a little peace knowing your love is always near
You can rest easy knowing your suffering is over
And it's okay we are sad but we knew it was time
I love you forever little auntie of mines

Whitney Hodge

Auntie Shannon

I never got to thank you for
everything you did for me,
And all the things you showed me.
I am grateful for all the
conversations we had.
I'm going to miss you fussing at me
about taking my medicine!!
All the times we stayed at the office
until 4am doing taxes!
I love you **soooo** much auntie,
and I will miss you forever.
I will keep my attitude in check.

Death

DEATH came in a stole my joy,
He took my love,
Love that I wasn't ready to let go of.
And all he left me was grief, and if you've never felt grief,
It feels like losing a game you didn't even know you were playing,
It feels like that feeling in your stomach when you were
on your way home knowing your teacher already called your mom.
It feels like every break up you've ever been in all rolled up in one.
It feels like a puzzle with missing pieces, like a IKEA dresser with no instructions,
A keyboard with no keys
It feels like a winter with no breeze.
It feels like **ME,** Broken, lost, confused
Like I'm pouring my heart out on Instagram with no views,
I feel weak
But I'm putting me back together again
I found new pieces to this old puzzle, and
No they cannot replace the old ones but maybe they can fill
The void and hold me together until I get

some instructions.
Hopefully they're coming before my destruction.
I'm praying they're coming soon!

Lucky Little Me

5 foot 4 and 5 foot 3 that's my mother and me
ME 5 foot 3 how lucky could I be
With Mother so kind and a mother so Wise
A woman so brave to leave all her fears behind
Through the struggle and the pain you never gave up
With faith the size of a mustard seed you never lost your trust
With a wardrobe so clean you never lost your touch
With all the burdens that was given you never said enough is enough
Never seen you cry when we was rough
Never seen you throw in the towel when things got tuff
 And for that I give you all my love and all my respects
When looking for a role model never had to look far cause you are the best
She's shouldered cry on when things are going wrong
She's got my back whenever I call and for that I'm strong
She lost her father and lost her mother

so she's s her sister's keeper and
She take care of her Brothers
I know Ma Daddy and Ma mama is saying
well done shawty for holding it down
And Donna left you with Courtney cause
she knew you were a mother who could
carry the Crown
cause you are her sister and you never let
her down and
Some may call you sister
Some may call you friend
Some may call you Auntie
Some may call you kin
But me I'm 5 foot 3
And how lucky could I be
To only be 1 of 3 to say you're a Mother to
me

A Letter To My Depression And Anxiety

Do you know how hard it was
for me to fix me?
Do you know how long it took?
Do you know how many pieces that were
missing from this puzzle?
I had to search far and wide to find these.
And I came to far to go back now
And I cried for this
And I prayed for this
And I almost died for this
And after years of trying with no
instructions with little to no help
I'm finally free
I'm finally happy
I'm finally ME
I did it
I found it
I conquered it
I mastered ME
I fixed ME
I love ME
I trust ME
And there's nothing you can do to take this
JOY from me

Whitney Hodge

So this is GOODBYE
I don't wish you well
And it WASN'T a pleasure meeting you

Love:

Whitney

The Reflections Of A Bruised Heart

I always wanted someone who could love me completely
Despite my flaws and iniquities
Someone who would value me
Understand me
Cherish me
Who Gets me
Someone to dance with
Laugh with
Cry with
Someone understanding and that has patience
A teacher
A friend
A partner
Someone to fight with just to make up
Someone who love the way we love
A person who Challenges me
A listener
A shoulder to cry
I have always wanted someone who loved me the way you do
I've always wanted YOU

Whitney Hodge

Story Time

A young lady walks into A ER hunched over in pain bruises on her neck and body a few on her waist close to her veins. You can look into her eyes and tell she's a bit insane She stops she yells,

"I need a DR. I need help somebody stop the pain"

The nurses came running and a doctor c came too. A old black man he grab her by the hand and said,

"Tell me miss what happened, how can I help you"

She looks at him straight in the eyes and said,

"I'm hurting, I'm hurting can u stop the pain it hurts on the inside I'm just not the same"

He said, *"Ok ma'am can u describe the pain"*

She starts to cry while holding her chest she says,

"I'm hurting doctor I'm hurting Doctor the pain is in my chest but it's only on the left side right under my breast, my stomach is sick and it

keep turning flips, I haven't ate in days I have lost 8 lbs. this is a trip"

"Ma'am we're going to see what we can do is that the only place that's boring you" the young nurse says,

"Don't forget my head. It aches in pain. I can't sleep at night, and that is a shame because I love to sleep. I keep having this vision of killing myself before midnight. So every night before the clock strikes 12, I tie my hands together until the sun comes up or until I get right. Sometimes this lasts until the next day at midnight." The doctor decides to run some tests, so he can decide what is best.

An hour later the doctor comes into the room where the young lady sits holding her chest. He looks at her and says,

"Ok ma'am. You had an EKG, a MRI, a X-Ray, an ultrasound, and some blood work done. The only problem is that we found none. According to your Labs, you're as healthy as can be. I'm sorry, but I have to ask is there something you're not telling me?"

She yells, *"I'm hurting I'm hurting can u stop the pain?! It hurts on the inside I'm just not the same!"*

He says,
"Yes, I know, and I heard it before. These

symptoms are too familiar. I had a daughter your age that went through the same thing except it killed her. We caught it too late and the pain was too great. These bruises on your body. How did you get this way?"

The girl looks up as if she woke up. Then, her eyes glazed over and she drafted into space. She opened up her mouth and she started to say

"It was entirely fault. I should've never left him alone. He said I'm the one to blame for going through his phone. But how was I to know he had several different females inside my home? He took my heart and now he's gone."

She stops talking, places her hands on her head, and says,

"Tell me, Doctor, what is this pain? Please tell me why am I not the same."

He looks at her and he sees her pain, but it's nothing he can do if she won't explain.

"Did you and this guy have a fight?" He asked.
She stops crying almost immediately. Her eyes turned red as can be. At this moment, the doctor knew this was the last place he wanted to be. Seeing his daughter die of a broken heart by her own hand all over a man, and this girl was bringing back old

memories and that wasn't in today's plan. She stands to her feet she yells,

"How could he do this to me? He was supposed to protect me from all harmful things. Little did I know he was the only harmful thing I needed protection from. Why didn't I run? Because he wasn't a thug and he didn't sell drugs. He didn't own a gun and wasn't a bum. He beat me until I was numb. then he picked me up and cleaned me up. He told me he loved me and he was sorry."

"Did you press charges?"

The doctor Interrupted. The girl became very calm, she says,

"Love don't hurt. Love don't grab you by the throat and squeeze and let go right before the life leave your eyes. I cried and cried and he stayed by my side he said and told me never to question him again. And at that moment I know this had to end, but I still loved him deep within. I knew I couldn't win."

"What happened Miss?"

The doctor asked. She looks him in the eyes and says,

"I'm hurting! I'm hurting! Can u stop the pain? It hurts on the inside! I'm just not the same. He came into my life and he made me

whole. He took my heart so I took his soul."

THE END

About the Author

Whitney Hodge, a native of Fort Worth, Tx, is a talented poet, author, and motivator. She uses her intuition and life experience to relate to her audience with great transparency. Her debut piece of work entitled "No Love Lost" captivated it's audience and continues to sell today.

She is a member and an advocate for the LGBTQ community, and is a forerunner for all social advancement and injustices. Whitney will not only blow you away with her amazing skill, but will capture your heart with every turn of the page. She displays love, compassion, and integrity in every way.

Get connected with
Author Whitney Hodge on social media

 Whitney Hodge and No Love Lost

 _imtheproblem_

The Reflections Of A Bruised Heart

www.ingramcontent.com/pod-product-compliance
Lightning Source LLC
Chambersburg PA
CBHW071509070526
44578CB00001B/488